Stories with a View: Narrative Inspirations

~ Selected Poetry and Paintings ~
Story starters for Grades 3-6

Margot Davidson

Copyright©2004 Margot Davidson
Hillside Education
475 Bidwell Hill Road
Lake Ariel, PA 18436

All artwork in this publication is used by license agreement with Art Resource, Inc. Please do not reproduce the paintings by any media. Please do not reproduce any part of this book without written permission of the author.

Photo Credits

Credit: **Art Resource, NY**
Maurice Pendergast, *The Fairgrounds*

Credit: **Fine Art Photographic Library, London/Art Resource, NY**
Joseph Clark, *Playing with the Kittens*
John Emms, *A Restful Tune*
Robert Farrier, *Feeding the Rabbits*
Myles Birket Foster, *The Entangled Kite* and *Maiden Voyage*
Adolf Heinrich Lier, *Winter Scene with Children Playing*
William Muckley, *Holiday Riots or The Muckley Children at Play*
Caroline Paterson, *Captured Unawares*

Credit: **Giraudon/Art Resource, NY**
Berthe Morisot, *Eugene Manet and his Daughter at Bougival*

Credit: **Smithsonian American Art Museum, Washington DC/Art Resource, NY**
George Catlin, *Buffalo Chase, A Single Death*

Credit: **Scala/Art Resource, NY**
Giacomon Ceruti, *Boy with a Basket*
Giacomo Favretto, *The Mouse*
Girolamo Induno, *Childhood Mishaps*
Francisco de Goya y Lucientes, *Two Children with Their Dog*
Filippo Palizzi, *Street Urchins*

Credit: **Victoria and Albert Museum, London/Art Resource, NY**
Kronheim & Co., *Children's Pastimes on the Beach*
William Mulready, *A Sailing Match*

Guide to *Stories with a View*

To the Teacher

This collection is intended as a supplement to your regular language arts program. The selected pieces and the accompanying discussion questions are designed to inspire narration, written or oral. This collection may be used once a week for a year or twice a month for two years, perhaps as a Friday break. The poetry may also be used for copywork or memorization, or just for fun reading. The poems and paintings may be studied in any order, however, some are related to each other by topic.

Recommended Procedure

Paintings

Direct the student to view the paintings and discuss the work using the provided questions. Encourage the student to ask his own questions about the painting as well. After discussing the painting, the student will write or dictate a story suggested by the painting.

Unused to this type of writing, some students may merely describe the painting without telling a story.

Example: *There is a dog. Two boys are holding him. They are ten years old.*

To encourage **narration** instead, ask the student to start the story with *action* and tell what *happens*. A story has a beginning that introduces the setting and characters, a middle that tells the story in order, and a conclusion that ends the story satisfactorily, solving whatever problem the characters encountered in the story.

Example: *One day two boys named John and Roger got some food and went down the river in a boat. They looked forward to going to the island. When they got to the island, they unpacked and John looked off with his telescope. Roger got on his swimming shorts and went swimming. Then John got into his swimming shorts and went swimming.*

When they were swimming, Roger started diving. John said, "What are you diving for?"

"Pearls," Roger answered.
"Have you found any yet?" asked John.
"No, but I will," Roger answered.
"Are you sure there are any pearls here?"
"No but there might be."
Then they heard a noise in the woods of the island. They both got into their clothes and went into the woods to see what it was. Then they saw it. It was a bear, a big grizzly bear. It started to run at them. They turned around and ran back to the beach. But the bear chased them. They threw all their things in the boat and they rowed away as fast as they could.

When they got home, they told their mother and father, but they did not believe the boys. So the boys ate lunch and settled down to do their school for the next day. They agreed to go to a different island the next time.

(Dictated by a third grader, inspired by the painting
Two Boys Rowing by Winslow Homer.)

As an optional feature, story starter lines are provided below in the teaching tips specific to each work. You may suggest them to a student who is having trouble getting started.

Poetry

The student may read the poem on his own and then meet with the teacher to discuss the questions. However, the best method is that the teacher read the poem out loud to the child first. Then the student reads the poem alone or in chorus with the teacher. Discuss any unknown words and the provided discussion questions. Encourage the student to ask his own questions about the poem.

The student will then write a paragraph, story, or poem suggested by the poem. Sample first lines are provided in the teaching tips section below.

Example: *The rain pelted against my window and I knew the baseball game would be canceled. I heard it sloshing through the rain gutters on the roof and splashing into the gardens down below. Out my window, it looked like a sheet of water streaming past. Everything was grey and cold. I threw my glove on the bed and picked up a book to read.*

(Written by a fourth grader, inspired by the poem
"Rain in the Night" by Amelia Josephine Burr.)

Writing Folders and Portfolios

The student should keep all the things he writes in a *writing folder* or binder. Several times during the year, review the writing with the student and talk about the strengths of each piece. The student should then select the pieces he considers to be his best work and place them in a *writing portfolio*.

At the end of the year, repeat the process. Review what was placed in the portfolio earlier and compare those to the new pieces. Ask the student to design his portfolio the way that he likes best. He may design his collection based on the pieces he thinks represent his best effort, or the collection may be pieces that he *likes* the best, or the collection may represent a variety of genre and style. Only four or five pieces should end up in the portfolio.

This process is a great way to get the student thinking about his writing in a reflective and critical way. He should be able to tell you why he chose the pieces that he included and what the design of his collection is.

Publishing Student Work

You may choose to have your student dictate all the pieces that he writes. In that case, you could type them as he dictates and print them out to be placed in the writing folder. If he writes his own stories, consider all first attempts at narration as *first drafts*. You might consider filing some of these first drafts "as is" in the writing folder. For other first drafts, you may ask the student to complete the writing process and produce a corrected final copy. To do this, the teacher discusses the narration with the student. Together the teacher and student decide on improvements that can be made to the first draft. The student then makes a final copy correcting any spelling and punctuation errors. These corrected drafts are placed in the writing portfolio.

You may want to ask the student to illustrate the story that he writes. Any narration may also be made into a book with a series of illustrations. As a fun variation, ask the student to draw a series of pictures first and then use them to tell the story.

Teaching Tips For Each Work

1. "Trees" by Joyce Kilmer

This poem is a series of couplets. Couplets are two lines of poetry which rhyme. This kind of poem is easy for children to write and perhaps your student could experiment with writing just two lines of verse about many different things in creation.

Sample: I spied a shiny rock today
      As I marched along my way.

Sample: I went skipping to the stream
      And laying down I had a dream.

2. *The Mouse* by Giacomo Favretto

Story starter suggestions:
- The girls screamed as George opened the door.
- That mouse was on the loose again!

3. "Lone Dog" by Irene Rutherford McLeod

Sample first lines:
- My aunt has a dog named Sadie. She is old and thick.
- Our dog Moseby was the best dog we ever had.

4. *Two Children with Their Dog* by Francisco Goya y Lucientes

Story starter suggestions:
- The two boys stood wondering what to do.
- "You said I could ride him first," cried James to his brother.

5. "A Book" by Emily Dickinson

Framework for writing about a book:
    My favorite book is _____ by _____.
    I like it because _____ and _____.
    In this story . . .

6. *Feeding the Rabbits* by Robert Farrier

Story starter suggestions:
- Henry gazed lovingly at the rabbits.
- Every day Henry brought little scraps from the garden for the rabbits.
- Henry checked on Master Luke's rabbits every day.

7. "The Hens" by Elizabeth Madox Roberts

Sample first lines of a description of morning:
- The sun was rising over the hill and the air was fresh and very still.
- The hens were quiet and still. Suddenly the call of the rooster shattered the morning.

8. *Boy with a Basket* by Giacomon Cerutti

Story starter suggestions:
- Sancho left for market very early in the morning.
- All week Sancho had been thinking about market day.

9. "Daisies" by Bliss Carman

Sample first lines:
- Wildflowers grow all along the side of our road.
- Grandma's roses are the prettiest I've ever seen.
- A forget-me-not is my favorite flower.

10. *Street Urchins* by Filippo Palizzi

Story starter suggestions:
- The boys on Samson Street were always teasing Mr. Larson's donkey.
- Mickey called the other boys when he saw Mr. Larson's donkey gallop down the street.
- Mr. Larson's donkey was loose again!

11. "A Little Song of Life" by Lizette Woodworth Reese

Sample first lines:
- I'm glad that I live in Texas.
- I'm glad that God loves me.
- I'm glad that I have a big brother.

12. *Buffalo Chase, A Single Death* by George Catlin

Story starter suggestions:
- The tribe had been planning a buffalo hunt since the snow first began to melt.
- Little Turtle checked his bow as he prepared for the buffalo hunt.

13. "The Shepherd Boy" by Maud Keary

Sample of the first two lines of a third stanza for the poem:
The sheep around him eat and sleep,
  They never have a care.

Sample first line of a description of the boy:
Bill, the shepherd boy works all day in the hills. He whistles as he gathers the sheep up.

14. *A Restful Tune* by John Emms

Story starter suggestions:
- Johnny rested on the hill as the sheep grazed nearby.
- The sheep dogs rested from their work as Johnny played a sweet tune for them on his whistle.
- The morning sun beat down on the lonely hillside and Johnny couldn't wait until it was time for lunch.

15. "In the Bleak Midwinter" by Christina Rossetti

This poem has been set to music, and you may find it in a Christmas carol book. The music is beautiful and melancholy, with a touch of crescendo here and there to make it a most excellent Advent/Christmas meditation.

    Do all that you can to encourage the child to write about his own gift to God; it will be much more special. Children are usually pretty good at composing prayers. Use the sample first lines below only if he is really stuck.

Sample first lines:
- My God I give you my heart
- Baby Jesus, so small and dear
- All I have I give to you, Dear Lord

16. *Holiday Riots or The Muckley Children at Play* by William Muckley

Story starter suggestions:
- Sandra screamed as Roger leveled his musket at the captive.
- After a lovely holiday dinner, the children went to play with their new toys.

17. "At the Aquarium" by Max Eastman

Sample first lines:
- I watched the people as they passed by my home.
- The big tunas shoved me as I tried to peer through the seaweed at the strange creatures just beyond us.

18. *Winter Scene with Children* by Adolf Heinrich Lier

Story starter suggestions:
- All the school children planned to meet after Christmas for a day of sledding.
- "Hello!" called Carl as the Gibbon family joined them at the frozen creek.

19. "Where Go the Boats" by Robert Louis Stevenson

Sample first lines:
- As the little boat traveled down the river, it saw many strange sights along the way.
- "There goes my boat!" cried Andy as it slipped past the children by the side of the stream.
- A little boat floated past the children and picked up speed as it disappeared through the rocks.

20. *A Sailing Match* by William Mulready

Story starter suggestions:
- "There she blows!" called Edmund as his boat sailed past Peter's.
- Edmund and Peter were sailboat rivals.

21. "Home, Sweet Home" by John Howard Payne

Sample first lines:
- My home is the best place to be.
- At my house, everything is peaceful and fun.
- How would you like to visit the best place on the planet?

22. *Playing with the Kittens* by Joseph Clark

Story starter suggestions:
- Granny let the kittens come into the kitchen to play.
- Our cat, Matilda, had kittens a few weeks ago.
- My kitten jumped and scooted across the floor as she played with an empty spool.

23. "I Never Saw a Moor" by Emily Dickinson

Sample first lines of a description:

I have never seen the beach but I think I know how it would feel. The hot sand would burn my toes.

24. *Maiden Voyage* by Myles Birket Foster

Story starter suggestions:
- Gretchen and Rolf raced the twins to the stream.
- All winter, Rolf had been working on a new boat.
- Rolf held his breath as he set his new boat in the water. Would it float? Would it sail upright?

25. "From a Railway Carriage" by Robert Louis Stevenson

Sample first lines of a description from a train:
- While riding a train in Pennsylvania, I see hills and pine trees.
- From my window on the train, I see little houses and children playing.

26. *The Fairgrounds* by Maurice Pendergrast

Story starter suggestions:
- On a sunny day the park filled with children eager to ride the carousel.
- Grandma told me about the fairgrounds where she played as a girl.
- "I want to ride the boats first," exclaimed Hetty to her sister.

27. "The Steam Engine" by Maud Keary

Sample first lines of a description of a train going by:
- The metal carriage shook my house and I couldn't hear my brother calling to me.
- All of a sudden out of the mist, the great black engine came bursting into view.
- I counted the cars as the train sped past me.

28. *The Entangled Kite* by Myles Birket Foster

Story starter suggestions:
- Margie and Suzanne tramped through the woods and scrub brush until they reached the pasture.
- "Let's eat lunch first," said Mark as the children reached the top of the hillside.

29. "The Day Before April" by Mary Carolyn Davies

Sample first lines to a song about something in nature:
- I walk in the trees,
  I smell the sweet fresh leaves.

- Flowers blossom and bloom,
  Peepers sing a merry tune.
      (from "The Spring Poem" by Cecilia Davidson, 6 years old)

30. *Childhood Mishaps* by Girolamo Induno

Story starter suggestions:
- Pedro and Miguel had hiked all day to get to Marshy Creek.
- Just when they were about to turn homeward, the accident happened.

31. "Rain in the Night" by Amelia Josephine Burr

See the sample description inspired by this poem printed on page 39.

Other sample first lines:
- I heard the rain pattering on my window and knew the storm had begun.
- I love to sit inside on a rainy day and listen to the rain tapping on my roof.
- Dark clouds moved slowly overhead. I heard the clap of thunder.

32. *Captured Unaware* by Caroline Paterson

Story starter suggestions:
- Caroline had been waiting for the perfect time to play a trick on John.
- John snoozed happily on his chair.
- The children were tired of their lessons.

33. "The Elf and the Dormouse" by Oliver Herford

The invention the child describes does not have to be created by an animal or imaginary character as in this poem. Perhaps an accident caused an invention, or perhaps someone set out to invent one thing and came up with another. You may begin by having the student brainstorm ideas for things that have been invented that might have a silly story behind them.

Invention ideas:
- How the glue stick was invented.
- How a needle for sewing was invented.
- How the pencil was invented.

34. *Eugene Manet and his Daughter at Bougival* by Berthe Morisot

Bougival is a suburb of Paris. Many painters have used it as scenery for their paintings. (For example, Renoir: *Dance at Bougival;* Monet: *Bridge at Bougival.*)

Story starter suggestions:
- Mary set her village on her Papa's lap.
- "Tell me a story about this little house, Papa," Mary asked.
- Mary and her Papa visited the gardens on the sunniest day of June.

35. "He Wishes for the Cloths of Heaven" by William Butler Yeats

Sample first lines:
- The most special gift I have ever given is . . . .
- I love to give a special gift to my mother every year.
- This year I would like to give my brother . . .

36. *Children's Pastime on the Beach* by Kronheim & Co.

Story starter suggestions:
- Amelia and Charles dug furiously at the sand.
- On the first day of spring, when the air was still chilly and damp, the children head to the beach beyond the fishing piers.
- Nellie and Kevin loved nothing better than to dig for treasures on the beach.

37. "The New Colossus" by Emma Lazarus

The author of this poem worked for many years to help Jewish immigrants who came to America after being persecuted in Russia in the 1800's.

Sample first lines of a letter:
- Dear America,
  I have seen many ships come into this harbor.
- Dear Mama,
  I have safely arrived. You would not believe all that has happened to me since I left home.

To The Student

The paintings and poetry in this book have been selected to inspire you to write stories, poems and descriptions. Most of the time you write, you write about things that you know or like, but perhaps the selections in this book will help you stretch a bit and use your imagination.

> A painter strives to represent
> The things he sees and feels,
> Telling a story through his painting
> To waiting eyes.
>
> The poet paints his life,
> His discoveries, with words,
> Expressing his feelings through imagery
> To waiting ears.

You, too, can create something that reflects your thoughts and feelings. Open your eyes and your heart and see what stories are waiting inside of you. Keep all your writing in a special folder or binder so you will have a record of all that you think about and write during the year.

> *So, whether you eat or drink, or whatever you do,*
> *do all to the glory of God.*
> 1 Corinthians 10:31

Poetry and Paintings

Trees

I think that I shall never see
A poem as lovely as a tree.

A tree whose hungry mouth is prest
Against the sweet earth's flowing breast;

A tree that looks at God all day,
And lifts her leafy arms to pray;

A tree that may in summer wear
A nest of robins in her hair;

Upon whose bosom snow has lain;
Who intimately lives with rain.

Poems are made by fools like me,
But only God can make a tree.
Joyce Kilmer

Assignment 1

"Trees" by Joyce Kilmer (1886-1918)

Discussion:
1. What is the poet saying about trees?
2. What is the poet saying about creation?
3. What does the poet mean when he says that the tree's hungry mouth is pressing against the earth?
4. Draw a picture of a tree.

Writing:
Write your own poem about trees or creation.

The Mouse
By Giacomo Favretto

Assignment 2

The Mouse by Giacomo Favretto (1849-1887)
Pinacoteca di Brera, Milan, Italy

Discussion:
1. Where is the mouse in the painting?
2. Describe what is happening in the painting.
3. What kind of room is it?
4. What things in the painting give you clues about what room it is?
5. How do the people in the painting feel? How can you tell?

Writing:
Write a story suggested by this painting.

Lone Dog

I'm a lean dog, a wild dog, and lone;
I'm a rough dog, a tough dog, hunting on my own;
I'm a bad dog, a mad dog, teasing silly sheep;
I love to sit and bay the moon, to keep fat souls
    from sleep.

I'll never be a lap dog, licking dirty feet,
A sleek dog, a meek dog, cringing for my meat,
Not for me the fireside, the well-filled plate,
But shut door, and sharp stone, and cuff and kick
    and hate.

Not for me the other dogs, running by my side,
Some have run a short while, but none of them would bide.
O mine is still the lone trail, the hard trail, the best,
Wide wind, and wild stars, and hunger of the quest!
                           Irene Rutherford McLeod

Assignment 3

"The Lone Dog" by Irene Rutherford McLeod (1885-1977)

Discussion:
1. What breed of dog do you think the Lone Dog is?
2. Where might a dog like this live?
3. Do you think he could be someone's pet? Explain why or why not.
4. Do you think it is possible the author is writing about herself? Reread the poem with that possibility in mind and see what you think.
5. Draw a dog you think would fit this poem

Writing:
Describe a dog you have known or seen.

Two Children with Their Dog
By Francisco de Goya y Lucientes

Assignment 4

Two Children with Their Dog
By Francisco de Goya y Lucientes (1746-1828)
Museo del Prado, Madrid, Spain

Discussion:
1. What do you think the dog's name is?
2. What are the boys trying to do?
3. Who owns the dog?
4. Is he a friendly dog? How can you tell?

Writing:
Write a story about the boys and the dog.

A Book

There is no frigate like a book
    To take us lands away,
Nor any coursers like a page
    Of prancing poetry.

This traverse may the poorest take
    Without oppress of toil;
How frugal is the chariot
    That bears a human soul.
Emily Dickinson

Assignment 5

"A Book" by Emily Dickinson (1830-1886)

Vocabulary:
frigate – boat
coursers – horses
traverse – road, journey
frugal – not fancy, inexpensive

Discussion:
1. How does the author feel about books?
2. Who does she think may enjoy books?
3. According to the author, what can a book do for us?

Writing:
Tell about your favorite book and explain why you like it.

Feeding the Rabbits
By Robert Farrier

Assignment 6

Feeding the Rabbits by Robert Farrier (1769-1879)
Haynes Fine Art Gallery, Broadway, Great Britain

Discussion:
1. Where do you think this scene takes place?
2. How old is the boy in the painting?
3. What can you tell about the boy by his clothing?
4. Are the rabbits his pets? What clues in the painting help you to decide?

Writing:
Write a story about the boy and the rabbits in this painting.

The Hens

The night was coming very fast;
It reached the gate as I ran past.

The pigeons had gone to the tower of the church
And all the hens were on their perch.

Up in the barn, and I thought I heard
A piece of a little purring word.

I stopped inside, waiting and staying,
To try and hear what the hens were saying.

They were asking something, that was plain,
Asking it over and over again.

One of them moved and turned around,
Her feathers made a ruffled sound,

A ruffled sound like a bushful of birds,
And she said her little asking words.

She pushed her head close in her wing,
But nothing answered anything.

Elizabeth Madox Roberts

Assignment 7

"The Hens" by Elizabeth Madox Roberts (1881-1941)

Discussion:
1. What time of day is the author writing about? How can you tell?
2. What sound do you think the hens are making?
3. What does the author mean when she says that they were asking something over and over again?

Writing:
Describe the morning when the hens awake.

Boy with a Basket
By Giacomon Ceruti

Assignment 8

Boy with a Basket by Giacomon Ceruti (c.1700-c.1768)
Pinacoteca di Brera, Milan, Italy

Discussion:
1. Who is the boy? Where does he live?
2. What do you think he is doing with the eggs and chicken?
3. What do you think the big basket is for?
4. Do you think he is going somewhere or coming home?

Writing:
Write a story suggested by this painting.

Daisies

Over the shoulders and slopes of the dune
I saw the white daisies go down to the sea,
A host in the sunshine, an army in June,
The people God sends us to set our hearts free.

The bobolinks rallied them up from the dell,
The orioles whistled them out of the wood;
And all of their singing was, "Earth, it is well!"
And all of their dancing was, "Life, thou art good!"
Bliss Carman

Assignment 9

"The Daisies" by Bliss Carmen (1861-1929)

Discussion:
1. Read the poem again and notice where it rhymes.
2. Why do you think the author calls the daisies people?
3. How do the daisies make the author feel? What words in the poem let you know how the author feels about them?
4. Who is singing and dancing in the poem?
5. Why do you think the author includes birds in a poem about daisies?

Writing:
Write a description of flowers that you have seen or like especially. Make it into a poem if you like.

Street Urchins
By Filippo Palizzi

Assignment 10

Street Urchins by Filippo Palizzi (1818-1899)
Galleria d'Arte Moderna, Florence, Italy

Discussion:
1. Why do you think the boys are chasing the donkey? See if you can think of two or three different reasons.
2. Where does the scene take place?
3. What is the small boy in the painting carrying?
4. Why do you think the boy in front falls?
5. What do you think the donkey might be feeling?

Writing:
Write a story suggested by the painting.
You may write it from the point of view of the donkey, the little dog, or the boys.

A Little Song of Life

Glad that I live am I;
That the sky is blue;
Glad for the country lanes,
And the fall of dew.

After the sun the rain,
After the rain the sun;
This is the way of life
Till all the work be done.

All that we need to do,
Be we low or high,
Is to see that we grow
Nearer the sky.
      Lizette Woodworth Reese

Assignment 11

"A Little Song of Life" by Lizette Woodworth Reese
(1856-1935)

Discussion:
1. What do you think the poet is trying to say about life in this poem?
2. Do you agree with her thoughts about life? Explain why or why not?
3. Which stanza talks about the cycle of life? What words does the author use to show the cycle of life?
4. What lines do you like best in this poem?

Writing:
Describe three things that make you glad.
Make it into a poem if you like.

Buffalo Chase, A Single Death
By George Catlin

Assignment 12

Buffalo Chase, A Single Death by George Catlin
(1796-1872)
Smithsonian American Art Museum, Washington DC, USA

Discussion:
1. Where does this scene take place?
2. Why do you think it is called "A Single Death"?
3. What do you think will happen next?

Writing:
Write a story suggested by this painting.

The Shepherd Boy

The farmer's shepherd boy is Bill:
    Across the fields he drives the sheep,
And where the long road winds uphill,
    Like little summer clouds they creep.

And Bill is like the gentle wind,
    He whistles softly as he goes,
He calls them where he has a mind,
    And never uses threats or blows.
              Maud Keary

Assignment 13

"The Shepherd Boy" by Maud Keary

Discussion:
1. Describe this shepherd boy in your own words.
2. Do you think that the sheep respond well to him? Why or why not?
3. What else would you like to know about the shepherd boy described in this poem?
4. Find the places in the poem where the lines rhyme.
5. Look at the picture of the shepherd boy on the next page. Do you think this poem could describe the boy in that picture? Why or why not?

Writing:
Make up another verse for this poem about the shepherd boy.
Or, write a description of the boy in your own words.

A Restful Tune
By John Emms

Assignment 14

A Restful Tune by John Emms (1843-1912)
Picton House Gallery, Broadway, Great Britain

Discussion
1. Describe where this scene takes place.
2. Who is the boy?
3. What time of day do you think it is?
4. What are the sheep doing while the dogs rest?

Writing:
Write a story about the boy and his dogs and sheep.

In the Bleak Midwinter

In the bleak midwinter, frosty winds made moan,
Earth stood hard as iron, water like a stone
Snow had fallen, snow on snow, snow on snow
In the bleak midwinter, long ago.

Our God, Heav'n cannot hold Him, nor earth sustain;
Heav'n and earth shall flee away when He comes to reign;
In the bleak midwinter a stable place sufficed
The Lord God Almighty, Jesus Christ.

Enough for Him, whom cherubim worship day and night,
A breastful of milk, and a mangerful of hay;
Enough for Him, Whom angels fall down before,
The ox and ass and camel which adore.

Angels and archangels may have gathered there,
Cherubim and seraphim thronged the air;
But only His mother in her maiden bliss
Worshipped the Beloved, with a kiss.

What can I give Him, poor as I am?
If I were a shepherd, I would give a lamb
If I were a wise man I would do my part –
Yet what I can I give Him, give my heart.
Christina Rossetti

Assignment 15

"In the Bleak Midwinter" by Christina Rossetti
(1830-1894)

Discussion:
1. Tell the meaning of each stanza of the poem.
2. What do you think is the main idea of the whole poem?
3. What is your favorite part of the poem?
4. How does the author give her gift to the newborn King?

Writing:
Write about a gift you would give or have given to Our Lord. You may write it as a poem.

Holiday Riots
or The Muckley Children at Play
By William Muckley

Assignment 16

Holiday Riots or The Muckley Children at Play
by William Muckley (1837-1905)
Galerie George

Discussion:
1. Look very carefully at the children in the picture.
2. What is each group of children doing?
3. What do you imagine the girl in the yellow dress is saying?
4. What holiday do you think it is?

Writing:
Write a story to accompany this picture.

At the Aquarium

Serene the silver fishes glide,
Stern-lipped, and pale, and wonder-eyed!
As through the aged deeps of ocean,
They glide with wan and wavy motion.
They have no pathway where they go,
They flow like water to and fro,
They watch with never-winking eyes,
They watch with staring, cold surprise,
The level people in the air,
The people peering, peering there:
Who wander also to and fro,
And know not why or where they go,
Yet have a wonder in their eyes,
Sometimes a pale and cold surprise.
Max Eastman

Assignment 17

"At the Aquarium" by Max Eastman (1883-1969)

Discussion:
1. What are your favorite lines of the poem?
2. How does the author compare the fish in the aquarium to the people who come to watch them?
3. What is the main idea of the poem?
4. Draw a picture of a scene from an aquarium.

Writing:
Imagine you are a fish and write about the people you see at the aquarium.

Winter Scene with Children Playing
By Adolf Heinrich Lier

Assignment 18

Winter Scene with Children Playing by Adolf Heinrich Lier (1826-1882)
Coll. Bubenik

Discussion:
1. Where does this scene take place?
2. What are the children in the painting doing?
3. What time of the day do you think it is?
4. What do you think is the mood of this painting? How does the painter use color and shadow to show the mood?

Writing:
Write a story about the children in this painting.

Where Go the Boats

Dark brown is the river,
    Golden is the sand.
It flows along forever,
    With trees on either hand.

Green leaves a-floating,
    Castles of the foam,
Boats of mine a-boating –
    Where will all come home?

On goes the river
    And out past the mill,
Away down the valley,
    Away down the hill.

Away down the river,
    A hundred miles or more,
Other little children
    Shall bring my boats ashore.
          Robert Louis Stevenson

Assignment 19

"Where Go the Boats" by Robert Louis Stevenson (1850-1894)

Discussion:
1. What is your favorite part of this poem?
2. Where does the author imagine that the river flows?
3. Why will some other children bring his boats ashore?
4. Draw a picture of the river scene.

Writing:
Describe a stream, river, or lake you have seen.
Or, tell the story of the boat that travels down a river and all that it sees.

A Sailing Match
By William Mulready

Assignment 20

A Sailing Match by William Mulready (1786-1863)
Victoria and Albert Museum, London, Great Britain

Discussion:
1. What do you think is happening in this picture?
2. What is the boy in the background doing?
3. What is the woman in the painting doing? Why do you think she does that?
4. What is the boy holding the rolled up paper doing?

Writing:
Write a story suggested by this painting.

Home, Sweet Home

'Mid pleasures and palaces though we may roam,
Be it ever so humble, there's no place like home!
A charm from the sky seems to hallow us there,
Which, seek through the world, is ne'er met with elsewhere!
    Home, Home! sweet, sweet home
        There's no place like home!
        There's no place like home!

An exile from home, splendor dazzles in vain.
Oh, give me my lowly thatch'd cottage again!
The birds singing gaily, that came at my call, --
Give me them, -- and the peace of mind dearer than all!
    Home, Home! sweet, sweet home
        There's no place like home!
        There's no place like home!
                John Howard Payne

Assignment 21

"Home, Sweet Home" by John Howard Payne (1791-1852)

Discussion:
1. How does the author feel about his home? What words or phrases show this?
2. Notice and point out where the poem rhymes.
3. Look at the painting on the page 48.
   Could that painting be used to illustrate the poem? Why or why not?
4. Is there one line from the poem that might be used as a caption for the painting?

Writing:
Write about how you feel about your home.

Playing with the Kittens
By Joseph Clark

Assignment 22

Playing with the Kittens by Joseph Clark (1834-1926)
Haynes Fine Art Gallery, Broadway, Great Britain

Discussion:
1. How are the people in this painting related?
2. What gives the painting a homey feeling?
3. What do you think the old woman has on her lap?
4. How is this kitchen the same as or different than yours?

Writing:
Write a story suggested by this painting.

I Never Saw a Moor

I never saw a moor,
I never saw the sea;
Yet know I how the heather looks,
And what a wave must be.

I never spoke with God,
Nor visited heaven;
Yet I am certain of the spot
As if the chart were given.
Emily Dickinson

Assignment 23

"I Never Saw a Moor" by Emily Dickinson (1830-1886)

Discussion:
1. How does the author show that she believes in God?
2. What other things does she believe in that she has never seen?
3. How does she know about the other things if she has never seen them?
4. Are there things you believe in even though you have not seen them?

Writing:
Write about something you've never seen, but have imagined.

Maiden Voyage
By Myles Birket Foster

Assignment 24

Maiden Voyage by Myles Birket Foster (1825-1899)
Private Collection

Discussion:
1. Compare this painting to *A Sailing Match* on page 44. How are they the same or different?
2. In what country do you think the children live?
3. In what time period do you think the painting is set?

Writing:
Write a story about the children and their boats in this painting.

From a Railway Carriage

Faster than fairies, faster than witches
Bridges and houses, hedges and ditches;
And charging along like troops in a battle,
All through the meadows the horses and cattle;
All the sights of the hill and the plain
Fly as thick as driving rain;
And every again in the wink of an eye,
Painted stations whistle by.

Here is a child who clambers and scrambles,
All by himself and gathering brambles;
Here is a tramp who stands and gazes;
And there is the green for stringing daisies!
Here is a cart run away in the road
Lumping along with man and load;
And here is a mill and there is a river:
Each a glimpse and gone for ever!
Robert Louis Stevenson

Assignment 25

"From a Railway Carriage" by Robert Louis Stevenson (1850-1894)

Discussion:
1. What is the author describing? Where is he when he sees these scenes?
2. List the things he sees as he passes.
3. How fast do you think the train is going?
4. Draw one of the scenes the author sees.

Writing:
Write a description of what you would see if you were on a train passing through the town or countryside in which you live.

The Fairgrounds
By Maurice Pendergast

Assignment 26

The Fairgrounds by Maurice Pendergast (1859-1924)
Private Collection

Discussion:
1. Notice and describe all the different things that the children are doing in this painting.
2. Which of the activities portrayed do you like best?
3. Is the scene in this painting similar to a fair you have seen? Explain how it is different or the same.
4. How do the colors add to the action of the picture?

Writing:
Write a story suggested by this painting.

The Steam-Engine

Through the night and through the day
The great steam-engine wends his way:
Unswerving, swift, he shall not stay
Through labyrinths of metal thread
Their shining lines before him spread,
And lights are changing green and red!

The great steam-engine tears along,
Of iron and flame, broad-breasted, strong,
His speed is as the eagle's, on
Past startled plain and mountain-height,
This bold embodiment of might
With flame and thunder rends the night!
Maud Keary

Assignment 27

"The Steam-Engine" by Maud Keary

Vocabulary:
wends – to proceed on one's way
rends – to rip or split apart
embodiment – physical representation of something

Discussion:
1. What does the author think of trains? (What is the main idea of the poem?)
2. Compare this poem to "From a Railway Carriage" on page 54.
    What is similar or different about them?
3. Notice and point out where the poem rhymes.

Writing:
Write your own description of a train passing by.

The Entangled Kite
By Myles Birket Foster

Assignment 28

The Entangled Kite by Myles Birket Foster (1825-1899)
Polak Gallery, London, Great Britain

Discussion:
1. Where does this scene take place and at what time of the year?
2. How old do you think each of the children is?
3. Do you think they are related to each other? If so, how are they related?
4. Whose kite do you think it is? What clues help you to decide?

Writing:
Write a story about the children in the painting and their kite.

The Day Before April

The day before April
    Alone, alone,
I walked in the woods
    And sat on a stone.

I sat on a broad stone
    And sang to the birds.
The tune was God's making
    But I made the words.
        Mary Carolyn Davies

Assignment 29

"The Day Before April" by Mary Carolyn Davies
(fl.1914-1929)

Discussion:
1. Why do you think she says the tune is God's making?
2. What kinds of birds sing where you live?
3. What is the weather like the day before April? Describe it.
4. Draw a picture of the scene described in the poem.

Writing:
Write the words to a song about walking in nature.
Or, describe the birds in your neighborhood.

Childhood Mishaps
By Girolamo Induno

Assignment 30

Childhood Mishaps by Girolamo Induno (1825-1890)
Galleria d'Arte Moderna di Nervi, Genoa, Italy

Discussion:
1. Where does this scene take place?
2. What do you think the "mishap" is?
3. Who are the boys? Where do they live?
4. What time of day is it? How can you tell?

Writing:
Write a story about the scene in this picture.

Rain in the Night

Raining, raining,
   All night long;
Sometimes loud, sometimes soft,
   Just like a song.

There'll be rivers in the gutter
   And lakes along the street.
It will make our lazy kitty
   Wash his little dirty feet.

The roses will wear diamonds
   Like king and queens at court;
But the pansies all get muddy
   Because they are so short.

I'll sail my boat tomorrow
   In wonderful new places,
But first I'll take my watering pot
   And wash the pansies' faces.
          Amelia Josephine Burr

Assignment 31

"Rain in the Night" by Amelia Josephine Burr (1878-1900)

Discussion:
1. What are your favorite lines in this poem?
2. Why do the pansies need washing?
3. What does it sound like to you when it is rains at night?
4. What does it look like around your house after a rain?

Writing:
Describe a rainy day.

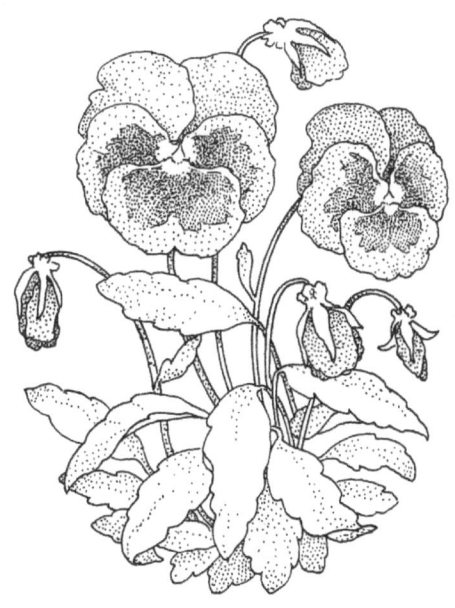

Captured Unawares
By Caroline Paterson

Assignment 32

Captured Unawares by Caroline Paterson (d.1919)
Haynes Fine Art Gallery, Broadway, Great Britain

Discussion:
1. Where do you think this scene takes place?
2. What does the boy have in his lap?
3. What does the girl use to tie him up?
4. What do you think the boy will do when he wakes up?

Writing:
Write a story to accompany this picture.

The Elf and the Dormouse

Under a toadstool crept a wee Elf,
Out of the rain to shelter himself.

Under the toadstool, sound asleep,
Sat a big Dormouse all in a heap.

Trembled the wee Elf, frightened, and yet
Fearing to fly away lest he get wet.

To the next shelter – maybe a mile!
Sudden the wee Elf smiled a wee smile,

Tugged till the toadstool toppled in two.
Holding it over him, gaily he flew.

Soon he was safe home, dry as could be.
Soon woke the Dormouse – "Good Gracious me!"

"Where is my toadstool?" loud he lamented.
– And that's how the umbrella was invented.

Oliver Herford

Assignment 33

"The Elf and the Dormouse" by Oliver Herford
(1863-1935)

Discussion:
1. Retell this story in your own words.
2. What do you think of the elf's behavior?
3. Why do you think he was afraid of the dormouse?
3. Draw a picture to accompany this poem.

Writing:
Write a story that explains another invention.

Eugene Manet and his Daughter at Bougival
By Berthe Morisot

Assignment 34

Eugene Manet and his Daughter at Bougival
By Berthe Morisot (1841-1895)
Private Collection, Paris, France

Discussion:
1. What do you think the girl is playing with?
2. What do you think "Bougival" is?
3. What kind of a day is it?
4. What mood does the artist portray by his use of color?

Writing:
Write a story about the painting. Be sure to describe Bougival.

He Wishes for the Cloths of Heaven

Had I the heavens' embroidered cloths,
Enwrought with golden and silver light,
The blue and the dim and the dark cloths
Of night and light and the half light,
I would spread the cloths under your feet:
But I being poor, have only my dreams;
I have spread my dreams under your feet;
Tread softly because you tread on my dreams.
William Butler Yeats

Assignment 35

"He Wishes for the Cloths of Heaven"
by William Butler Yeats (1865-1939)

Discussion:
1. What do you think the poet is trying to say? (What is his main idea?)
2. To whom do you think the poet is speaking?
3. What does he wish to give? Why does he want to give this gift?
4. Do you think giving someone your dreams is a good gift? Explain.
5. Compare this poem to "In the Bleak Midwinter" on page 34. Is there anything similar about them? What is different about them?

Writing:
Write about giving a special gift to someone.

Children's Pastime on the Beach
By Kronheim & Co.

Assignment 36

Children's Pastime on the Beach by Kronheim & Co.
(19th Century)
Victoria and Albert Museum, London, Great Britain

Discussion:
1. Where does this scene take place and at what time of the year? How can you tell?
2. What do you think the children are doing? Why are they digging?
3. What are the things in the background of the picture?
4. Who do you think the person in the background is? What do you think she is thinking?

Writing:
Write a story about these children at the beach.

The New Colossus

Not like the brazen giant of Greek fame,
With conquering limbs astride from land to land;
Here at our sea-washed, sunset gates shall stand
A mighty woman with a torch, whose flame
Is the imprisoned lightning, and her name
Mother of Exiles. From her beacon-hand
Glows world-wide welcome; her mild eyes command
The air-bridged harbor that twin cities frame.

"Keep, ancient lands, your storied pomp!" cries she
With silent lips. "Give me your tired, your poor,
Your huddled masses yearning to breathe free,
The wretched refuse of your teeming shore,
Send these, the homeless, tempest-tost to me:
I lift my lamp beside the golden door."

Emma Lazarus

Assignment 37

"The New Colossus" by Emma Lazarus (1849-1887)

Discussion:
1. This statue is named the New Colossus. The old Colossus to which the poem refers was a statue built by the Ancient Greeks, considered to be one of the seven wonders of the ancient world. It toppled into the sea and no one has ever found it.
2. The words of the last stanza which begin "Give me your tired, your poor," are inscribed on the base of the Statue of Liberty. What is the "Mother of Exiles" saying in this quote?
3. What do you think the "golden door" is?
4. How do you think immigrants who come to America feel when they see this statue?

Writing:
Write a letter to America from the statue.
Or, imagine that you are an immigrant who has just entered the United States. Write a letter to family back home telling them about your experience seeing the statue.

www.ingramcontent.com/pod-product-compliance
Lightning Source LLC
Chambersburg PA
CBHW042001150426
43194CB00002B/80